# LOW POINT
# pasta

### over 60 recipes low in Points

SIMON & SCHUSTER
A VIACOM COMPANY

Becky Johnson

First published in Great Britain by Simon & Schuster UK Ltd, 2000.
A Viacom Company.

This edition produced for The Book People Ltd,
Hall Wood Avenue, Haydock, St. Helens WA11 9UL

First published 2002
Reprinted 2003

Simon & Schuster UK Ltd.
Africa House
64-78 Kingsway
London WC2B 6AH

Photography: Steve Baxter
Styling: Marian Price
Food preparation: Jane Stevenson
Design: Jane Humphrey
Typesetting: Stylize Digital Artwork
Printed and bound in China

A CIP catalogue record for this book is available
from the British Library

ISBN 0 74323 939 3

Pictured on the front cover: Spaghetti Bolognese, page 26
Pictured on the back cover: Spicy Sausage Pasta, page 34

# contents

25

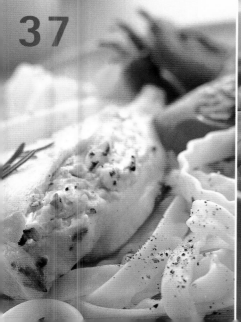

37

47

55

Popular with children and adults alike, pasta is the perfect food for busy Weight Watchers Members.

The recipes in this book, wisely used, make delicious, low calorie meals for the easiest ever weight loss. Pasta has the advantage that it fills you up without large quantities of fat or sugar.

The beauty of pasta is its versatility. It lends itself to so many different ingredients. These sauces are packed with full-bodied flavours and colours to excite both your taste buds and eyes. Most recipes take less than 20 minutes to prepare – turn to Super Quick and Easy Pasta (page 55) for recipes that are even quicker.

This book is a collection of favourite sauces that I have gathered on my travels, or from my work in hotels and restaurants or been given by family and friends. I hope that you enjoy them as much as I have over the years.

about
pasta

## TYPES OF PASTA

It is said that in Italy there are enough kinds of pasta to serve a different one every day. Here in the UK the choice may not be quite so extensive but there are still a great many types to choose from in our supermarkets, delicatessens and health food shops.

## SPECIALIST PASTA

The familiar wheatflour pastas are now available in organic and wholewheat versions from larger supermarkets, delicatessens and health food shops. Often the texture is very different from the more refined pastas but this can make a pleasant change. Wholewheat pasta is especially high in the B vitamins so often lacking in our diets.

There is also an increasing choice of wheat-free pastas becoming available, either for those with allergies or for the adventurous. These include: barley pasta; buckwheat pasta; corn and vegetable pasta (colourful pasta made from cornmeal with spinach, beetroot, tomato, celery and onion); rice pasta; and spelt pasta (spelt is a form of wheat).

## FLAVOURED PASTA

There is a wide choice of flavoured pasta. It is well worth exploring although the quality may vary.

*Basil:* dark green basil-flavoured pasta, good with most sauces.

*Black squid:* cuttlefish or squid ink is used to enrich the pasta. Has a slight seafood taste, so best served with fish or vegetable sauces.

*Porcini:* a distinctively flavoured, beige pasta made with Italian dried porcini (wild mushrooms).

*Smoked salmon:* orange pasta best used with plain, mild sauces.

*Spinach:* mildly flavoured, dark green pasta. Good with most sauces.

*Tomato, tomato and chilli, tomato and garlic:* these are pretty pink pastas. Plain tomato has a very mild flavour. Chilli and garlic give it more of a kick.

## COOKING PASTA

Disasters in cooking pasta are rare, but when they do happen, they are usually caused by one of three things:

1 Poor quality pasta. Some 'fresh pasta' can be of dubious quality. It absorbs a lot of water during cooking and becomes a soggy mass.

2 The pasta has been cooked and then reheated. Ideally, pasta needs to be cooked just before serving.

3 The pasta has been cooked incorrectly. Follow our method for perfect pasta every time.

## COOKING METHOD

Whether you are using fresh or dried, pasta needs plenty of boiling, salted water. Allow at least 1.5 litres (2¾ pints) for 350 g (12 oz) pasta and add a teaspoon of sea salt. Too little water and the pasta will stick to itself and the bottom of the pan.

Some people add a teaspoon of oil to the water to stop the pasta sticking to itself. Not only does the oil add Points, but I find that, if the pan is big enough and you stir the pasta 2–3 times during cooking, the pasta doesn't stick.

Some people prefer their pasta chewy, some softer. The only way to ensure that the pasta is properly cooked the way you like it, is to bite a bit of it a few minutes before the end of the cooking time.

1 Fill a large pan with water and add a teaspoon of salt. Bring the water to a fast boil. Or – and this is quicker – fill the kettle and bring it to the boil, then pour it straight into the pan, add the salt, replace the lid and bring to the boil once again. Remove the lid and add the pasta. Let spaghetti curl round the pan as it softens.

2 Stir once or twice to separate the pieces, but no more.

3 Simmer the pasta uncovered. Test after about three-quarters of the cooking time stated on the packet. Fresh pasta takes around 2–3 minutes; long, thin dried pasta about 5–8 minutes; thicker dried pasta shapes around 10 minutes.

4 Drain the pasta in a large colander. Never rinse pasta or you will remove the precious starch coating. Try to save a little of the cooking water as it is best for moistening the pasta or the sauce if either becomes too dry.

5 Return the pasta to the pan, add the sauce and toss, or place straight into a preheated serving dish and add the sauce on top to toss at the table.

**Spicy Beef Noodle Soup:** this beautiful soup is based on the clear, fragrant noodle soups found all over South East Asia.

# pasta soups & salads

From a hearty minestrone soup to a refreshing spring vegetable salad, this chapter contains easy to prepare snacks, suppers or starters to suit the season and your mood.

## SPICY BEEF NOODLE SOUP

**POINTS**

per serving: 5          per recipe: 19½

Serves 4
Preparation time: 10 minutes +
30 minutes marinating
Cooking time: 20 minutes
345 calories per serving
Freezing not recommended

250 g (9 oz) noodles
225 g (8 oz) beef steak, sliced thinly
200 g (7 oz) sugar snaps or mange-tout or green beans, sliced lengthways
1 pack of fresh coriander, chopped (optional)

FOR THE SOUP

2 litres (3½ pints) beef or chicken stock
1 garlic clove, smashed
1 lemongrass stick, chopped roughly, or 1 tablespoon dried lemongrass
1 small red chilli, de-seeded and chopped, or ½ teaspoon dried chilli flakes
1 star anise
1 cm (½ inch) fresh ginger, chopped, or 1 teaspoon ground ginger

FOR THE MARINADE

1 tablespoon soy sauce
1 garlic clove, chopped finely
2.5 cm (1 inch) fresh ginger, peeled and chopped finely
1 tablespoon honey
1 small red chilli, de-seeded and chopped finely, or ½ teaspoon dried chilli flakes

1  Place the soup ingredients in a saucepan and bring to the boil. Turn heat down to a simmer.

2  Cook the noodles.

3  Mix the marinade ingredients together in a shallow bowl and toss in the beef strips. Leave to marinate for up to 30 minutes.

4  Heat a frying-pan until very hot and then brown the steak strips for a minute on each side. Put on a plate to rest while you finish the soup.

5  Strain the soup, return to the pan and bring back to the boil. Throw in the sugar snaps, mange-tout or green beans for 2 minutes.

6  Divide the noodles between four serving bowls and add the beef.

7  Pour the soup over the noodles and beef. Serve sprinkled with chopped fresh coriander.

## MINESTRONE SOUP

**POINTS**

per serving: 3½          per recipe: 13½

Serves 4
Preparation time: 5 minutes
Cooking time: 20 minutes
240 calories per serving
Freezing recommended

This thick soup is the perfect, satisfying meal for those cold, dark winter days. Pasta such as little stars or shells or broken-up spaghetti or macaroni are suitable for this soup.

low-fat cooking spray
2 rashers rindless, unsmoked lean back bacon (about 25 g/1 oz each), chopped
2 onions, chopped roughly
2 garlic cloves, crushed
2 celery sticks, sliced thinly
2 litres (3½ pints) chicken stock
55 g (2 oz) pasta
300 g can borlotti or black-eye beans, drained
500 g (1 lb 2 oz) frozen mixed vegetables
400 g can chopped tomatoes
4 fresh sage leaves, chopped
salt and freshly ground black pepper

1  Spray a large frying-pan with cooking spray and fry the bacon over a high heat until it is crispy. Turn the heat down, add the onions, garlic and celery and cook until softened (about 5 minutes), stirring occasionally.

2  Pour in the stock and bring to the boil. Add the pasta, beans, mixed vegetables, tomatoes and fresh sage. Simmer for 15 minutes. Taste and season before serving.

## ITALIAN SOUP

Ⓥ Serves 4

*Preparation time: 10 minutes*
*145 calories per serving*
*Freezing recommended*

You can use any type of pasta for this including remnants from assorted half-empty packs.

| |
|---|
| 2 red peppers, chopped roughly |
| 2 green peppers, chopped roughly |
| ½ cucumber, peeled and chopped roughly |
| 1 red onion, chopped roughly |
| 2 garlic cloves, crushed |
| 200 g (7 oz) cooked pasta |
| 400 g can chopped tomatoes |
| 2 sprigs of fresh mint or 2 teaspoons dried mint |
| 2 tablespoons red wine vinegar |
| 1 tablespoon sugar |
| 1 yellow pepper, chopped finely |
| 2 fresh tomatoes, skinned, de-seeded and chopped finely |
| 1 pack of fresh parsley, chopped finely |
| salt and freshly ground black pepper |

1  Liquidise the red and green peppers, cucumber, onion, garlic, pasta, tomatoes, mint, vinegar, sugar and seasoning for a few seconds until you have a thick, soupy texture – not smooth. Pour into serving bowls and chill.

2  Garnish each bowl with some of the yellow pepper, fresh tomato and parsley, and possibly a couple of ice cubes, before serving.

COOK'S TIPS If you do not have a liquidiser then chop all the vegetables to a fine dice and mix with the other ingredients in a large bowl.

To skin and de-seed the tomatoes drop them into a bowl of boiling water for 10 seconds and then remove with a slotted spoon. The skins should slip off easily. If not then pop them back into the boiling water for another few seconds. Cut the tomatoes into quarters and remove the seeds.

VARIATION This soup can be served warm.

## PASTA, PORK AND BEAN SOUP

*Serves 4*
*Preparation time: 10 minutes*
*Cooking time: 10 minutes*
*345 calories per serving*
*Freezing recommended*

This is a lovely thick, comforting soup. The earthy flavour of rosemary perfectly complements the beans and pork. Any cut of pork will do as long as it is off the bone and lean.

| |
|---|
| low-fat cooking spray |
| 250 g (9 oz) cubed pork |
| 1 red onion, diced |
| 2 garlic cloves, crushed |
| 2 teaspoons dried rosemary or 2 tablespoons chopped fresh rosemary |
| 2 litres (3½ pints) chicken stock |
| 400 g can red kidney beans |
| 200 g (7 oz) pasta |
| salt and freshly ground black pepper |

1  Spray a large frying-pan with the cooking spray. Fry the pork over a high heat for 5 minutes or until golden brown. Add the onion, garlic, rosemary and seasoning. Stir-fry until softened – about 4 minutes.

2  Add the stock and bring to the boil. Add the beans and pasta and simmer for 10 minutes for small pasta, 15 minutes for larger pasta.

3  Pour the soup into a jug and liquidise in batches. Return the soup to the saucepan and check the seasoning before serving.

COOK'S TIPS You can, if you wish, use 50 g (1¾ oz ) dried beans. Soak them in plenty of water overnight. Cook them, again in plenty of water, without seasoning for 45 minutes after they have come to the boil.

**Italian Soup:
this soup is a
variation on the
classic summer
soup, gazpacho.**

## CHICKEN NOODLE SOUP

**POINTS**

| per serving: $4^{1}/_{2}$ | per recipe: 18 |
| --- | --- |

Serves 4
Preparation time: 5 minutes
Cooking time: 15 minutes
355 calories per serving
Freezing not recommended

This broth is well known all over the world for its comforting qualities. It's also a great way to use up leftover chicken.

low-fat cooking spray
2 onions, sliced thinly
2 garlic cloves, crushed
150 g (5½ oz) cooked chicken
2 litres (3½ pints) chicken stock
300 g (10½ oz) broken-up spaghetti or spaghettini
salt and freshly ground black pepper

1  Spray a large saucepan with the cooking spray, then put it on a high heat and stir-fry the onions and garlic for 2 minutes. Turn down the heat, put a lid on the saucepan and leave the onions and garlic to sweat for 10 minutes.

2  Add the chicken and stock and bring to the boil.

3  Add the pasta and simmer for 10 minutes. Check seasoning and serve.

COOK'S TIP To make a good, fresh chicken stock simply take a leftover chicken carcass. Remove any meat and reserve. Place the carcass in a large saucepan with a roughly chopped carrot, onion, celery stick, a couple of peeled and crushed garlic cloves, a bay leaf and some rosemary or thyme. Cover with water and simmer for 1½–2 hours. Occasionally skim off the fat with a spoon. Strain and keep in the fridge.

**Spring Vegetable and Pasta Salad:** warm, just-cooked, young vegetables and pasta tossed with fresh herbs and lemon.

## SPRING VEGETABLE AND PASTA SALAD

**POINTS**

| per serving: $3^{1}/_{2}$ | per recipe: $14^{1}/_{2}$ |
| --- | --- |

Ⓥ  Serves 4
Preparation time: 5 minutes
Cooking time: 15 minutes
320 calories per serving
Freezing not recommended

You can vary the herbs depending on what is available.

250 g (9 oz) pasta ribbons (tagliatelle, fettuccine)
150 g (5½ oz) mange-tout
150 g (5½ oz) baby carrots
250 g (9 oz) baby corns
175 g (6 oz) baby leeks
150 g (5½ oz) broccoli, chopped into florets

FOR THE DRESSING
juice and zest of 1 lemon
2 teaspoons extra-virgin olive oil
1 pack of fresh basil, torn up, or fresh coriander, chopped
1 pack of fresh chervil, chopped
1 pack of fresh parsley, chopped
1 teaspoon honey
salt and freshly ground black pepper

1  Bring 2 large pans of salted water to the boil. To one add the pasta and cook for 15 minutes or until done. Drain and place in a large serving bowl. To the other add the vegetables and cook until just done – about 3 minutes. Drain and add to the pasta.

2  In a bowl mix together all the dressing ingredients and pour over the warm vegetables and pasta. Toss and serve.

## PASTA, BROAD BEAN AND HAM SALAD

### POINTS

| | |
|---|---|
| per serving: 3 | per recipe: 12½ |

*Serves 4*
*Preparation time: 15 minutes*
*Cooking time: 12 minutes*
*160 calories per serving*
*Freezing not recommended*

*225 g (8 oz) fresh or frozen broad beans*
*225 g (8 oz) thick sliced, lean ham,*
*cut into 1 cm (½-inch) cubes*
*1 pack of fresh mint, chopped*
*175 g (6 oz) cooked pasta*

FOR THE DRESSING
*zest and juice of 1 lemon*
*1 teaspoon olive oil*
*1 teaspoon honey*
*1 teaspoon coarse-grain mustard*
*salt and freshly ground pepper*

1 Half fill a large pan with water and bring to the boil. Throw in the broad beans for 2 minutes and then drain. Run under cold water and drain again. Now the skins should just pop off when you squeeze the bean between thumb and forefinger. Put the bright green beans in a serving bowl with the ham, mint and cooked pasta.

2 Put all the dressing ingredients together in a jam jar, screw on the lid and shake vigorously. Pour over the pasta mix and toss.

COOK'S TIP The broad beans could be served whole but I prefer their texture and flavour if they are skinned.

## COTTAGE CHEESE AND VERMICELLI FRITTERS

### POINTS

| | |
|---|---|
| per serving: 4 | per recipe: 16 |

**V** *Serves 4*
*Preparation time: 15 minutes*
*Cooking time: 15 minutes*
*365 calories per serving*
*Freezing not recommended*

*3 eggs, separated*
*175 g (6 oz) vermicelli, broken up*
*and cooked*
*500 g (1 lb 2 oz) diet cottage cheese*
*a bunch of spring onions, chopped*
*finely*
*1 pack of chives, chopped*
*25 g (1 oz) plain flour*
*low-fat cooking spray*
*salt and freshly ground black pepper*

1 In a large bowl mix the egg yolks with the vermicelli, cottage cheese, spring onions, chives, flour and seasoning.

2 Whisk the egg whites until stiff and then fold into the cottage cheese mixture.

3 Spray a non-stick frying-pan with the cooking spray and place over a medium heat. Drop in spoonfuls of the mixture. Cook until the undersides are brown – about 6 minutes – and then turn with a fish slice and cook the other side.

4 Place on a tray lined with kitchen paper and keep warm in a low oven until the others are cooked.

**Cottage Cheese and Vermicelli Fritters: these low-fat fritters make a crispy and delicious starter or accompaniment.**

## SPICED TUNA AND PASTA SALAD

**POINTS**

| | |
|---|---|
| per serving: 1½ | per recipe: 7 |

*Serves 4*
*Preparation time: 5 minutes*
*140 calories per serving*
*Freezing not recommended*

A simple salad that's bursting with gutsy flavours. It's especially good with wholewheat pasta.

*198 g can tuna steak in brine*
*125 g (4½ oz) pasta shapes, cooked*
*450 g (1 lb) tomatoes, quartered and de-seeded*
*1 red onion, sliced finely*
*1 teaspoon chilli powder, or 1 fresh chilli, de-seeded and chopped finely*
*1 pack of fresh coriander, chopped*
*1 teaspoon ground cumin*
*2 teaspoons extra virgin olive oil*
*juice of 1 lemon*
*1 teaspoon sugar*
*salt and freshly ground black pepper*

1 Mix all the ingredients in a large bowl and serve.

## SPINACH PASTA SALAD WITH RED PEPPER DRESSING

**POINTS**

| | |
|---|---|
| per serving: 3 | per recipe: 12½ |

**V** *Serves 4*
*Preparation time: 15 minutes*
*Cooking time: 15 minutes*
*240 calories per serving*
*Freezing not recommended*

*150 g (5½ oz) spinach, tomato or plain pasta*
*200 g (7 oz) spinach, stems removed or baby spinach*
*100 g (3½ oz) low-fat soft cheese*
*1 tablespoon pine kernels, toasted (optional)*

FOR THE DRESSING

*2 red peppers*
*1 garlic clove, crushed*
*1 tablespoon balsamic vinegar or apple juice*
*1 teaspoon sugar*
*2 tablespoons water*
*salt and freshly ground black pepper*

1 Cook the pasta in plenty of salted, boiling water. Drain and immediately toss with the washed spinach in a large bowl. The heat from the pasta should just wilt the spinach.

2 Grill the red peppers until they are blackened on all sides and then place them in a plastic bag and leave until they are cool enough to handle. Peel away the charred skin, cut the peppers open and remove the seeds. Place the flesh in a liquidiser with the other dressing ingredients and process until smooth. Check the seasoning before pouring over the spinach and pasta.

3 Crumble the cheese on top of the salad and sprinkle with the pine kernels, if using.

**Spinach Pasta Salad with Red Pepper Dressing: a quick salad of bold flavours.**

**Cheese and Tuna Bake:** full of flavours your family love, this is a recipe you'll come back to time and time again.

We are always being told to eat more fish but where Weight Watchers Members are concerned this is especially important. Fish is the ultimate low-fat food that's high in protein and very satisfying. It's also a busy cook's best friend because it's extremely versatile and quick to prepare.

## SPAGHETTI MARINARA

**POINTS**

per serving: 5½        per recipe: 22½

Serves 4
Preparation time: 5 minutes
Cooking time: 30 minutes
505 calories per serving
Freezing not recommended

'Marinara' is an Italian word meaning 'of the sea'. You'll find it applied to all sorts of tuna-based sauces. This is one of the easiest.

low-fat cooking spray
2 onions, chopped
2 garlic cloves, chopped
2 x 400 g cans chopped tomatoes
2 teaspoons dried oregano (or 1 pack of fresh oregano, chopped)
1 teaspoon sugar
350 g (12 oz) spaghetti
2 x 200 g cans tuna steak in brine
4 tablespoons olives, pitted and chopped
salt and freshly ground black pepper

1  Spray a large frying-pan with the cooking spray. Heat the pan. Fry the onions and garlic until softened – about 4 minutes.

2  Add the tomatoes, oregano, sugar and seasoning and cook for 20 minutes, stirring occasionally.

3  Meanwhile cook the pasta in plenty of boiling, salted water, and then drain.

4  Add the tuna and olives and cook for a further 5 minutes. Check the seasoning and serve.

## CHEESE AND TUNA BAKE

**POINTS**

per serving: 7½        per recipe: 29½

Serves 4
Preparation time: 10 minutes
Cooking time: 30 minutes
490 calories per serving
Freezing not recommended

200 g (7 oz) pasta shapes
2 x 200 g cans tuna in brine
1 pack of fresh parsley, chopped
FOR THE SAUCE
2 tablespoons polyunsaturated margarine
2 tablespoons plain flour
600 ml (1 pint) skimmed milk
100 g (3½ oz) low-fat soft cheese
1 tablespoon French mustard
75 g (2¾ oz) half-fat Cheddar cheese, grated
salt and freshly ground black pepper

1  Cook the pasta in plenty of salted, boiling water for 10 minutes. Drain and place in an ovenproof dish. Add the tuna and parsley.

2  In a saucepan melt the margarine, stir in the flour and cook for 2 minutes. Gradually add the milk whisking all the time and bring the sauce to the boil. Simmer for 2 minutes, stirring and then stir in the soft cheese, mustard and seasoning.

3  Pour the sauce over the tuna and pasta and mix through. Sprinkle over the grated cheese and bake in the oven at Gas Mark 6/200°C/400°F for 20 minutes, or until golden and bubbling.

## ORIENTAL COD AND NOODLES

**POINTS**

per serving: 6½            per recipe: 27

*Serves 4*
*Preparation time: 5 minutes +*
*30 minutes marinating*
*Cooking time: 10 minutes*
*475 calories per serving*
*Freezing not recommended*

The cod remains moist on the inside while the outside is crisp. It's richly flavoured with soy and honey and served on a bed of stir-fried noodles with broccoli.

*4 x 200 g (7 oz) skinless cod steaks*

FOR THE MARINADE

*4 tablespoons soy sauce*

*2 tablespoons honey*

*4 tablespoons rice wine vinegar or white wine vinegar*

FOR THE STIR-FRY

*250 g (9 oz) noodles*

*low-fat cooking spray*

*1 teaspoon sesame oil*

*a bunch of spring onions, cut diagonally into 2.5 cm (1-inch) lengths*

*a head of broccoli, cut into florets*

*2 tablespoons sesame seeds, toasted*

1  Stir the marinade ingredients together in a shallow dish. Add the cod steaks and leave to marinate for up to ½ hour in the fridge.

2  Meanwhile cook the noodles. Drain, rinse and drain again.

3  Place the cod steaks under a high grill for about 5 minutes on each side or until cooked through.

4  Spray a large pan or wok with the cooking spray and place over a high heat. Add the sesame oil, spring onions and broccoli and toss for 3 minutes. Add the noodles, the leftover marinade and sesame seeds and stir-fry for a further 5 minutes.

5  Pile the noodles on serving plates and top with a cod steak.


## INDIAN SEAFOOD PASTA

**POINTS**

per serving: 5½            per recipe: 22

*Serves 4*
*Preparation time: 5 minutes*
*Cooking time: 25 minutes*
*420 calories per serving*
*Freezing not recommended*

This recipe borrows from the delicious creamy seafood curries that you find in Southern India.

*low-fat cooking spray*

*2 onions, chopped*

*2 garlic cloves, chopped*

*400 g (14 oz) seafood selection, fresh or frozen and defrosted*

*2 tablespoons curry paste*

*150 ml (¼ pint) fish or vegetable stock*

*400 g can chopped tomatoes*

*250 g (9 oz) noodles*

*1 pack of fresh coriander, chopped*

*250 g (9 oz) low-fat plain yogurt*

*salt and freshly ground black pepper*

1  Spray a large frying-pan or a wok with the cooking spray and put over a medium heat. Stir-fry the onions and garlic for 4 minutes or until soft. Add the seafood, curry paste, stock and tomatoes, and simmer for 20 minutes.

2  Cook the noodles in plenty of salted, boiling water for as long as stated on the packet.

3  Take the curry off the heat, check the seasoning and stir in the coriander and yogurt. Serve with the plain noodles.

COOK'S TIP For a more authentic curry flavour it is best to use whole spices like coriander seeds, cumin seeds, fennel seeds and turmeric. Grind them up in a food processor or in a pestle and mortar. Add a teaspoon of each spice to the curry, instead of the curry paste.

## LUXURIOUS SMOKED SALMON PASTA

**POINTS**

| per serving: $6^{1}/_{2}$ | per recipe: $26^{1}/_{2}$ |
|---|---|

*Serves 4*
*Preparation time: 5 minutes*
*Cooking time: 15 minutes*
*610 calories per serving*
*Freezing not recommended*

*240 g (8½ oz) pasta shapes or ribbons*
*300 g (10½ oz) smoked salmon*
*½ cucumber, diced finely*
*juice and zest of 1 lemon*
*150 g (5½ oz) very low-fat plain yogurt*
*50 g (1¾ oz) low-fat soft cheese*
*1 pack of fresh dill, chopped*
*salt and freshly ground black pepper*

1  Cook the pasta in plenty of salted, boiling water for 10–15 minutes then drain.
2  Cut the salmon into bite-sized pieces.
3  Add the salmon and other ingredients to the drained pasta and toss together.

## MONKFISH AND COCONUT CURRY

**POINTS**

| per serving: $8$ | per recipe: $32$ |
|---|---|

*Serves 4*
*Preparation time: 5 minutes*
*Cooking time: 35 minutes*
*495 calories per serving*
*Freezing recommended*

*low-fat cooking spray*
*2 onions, chopped roughly*
*400 g (14 oz) monkfish tails, cut into bite-sized pieces*
*2 tablespoons Thai green curry paste*
*175 g (6 oz) green beans, cut into 2.5 cm (1-inch) lengths*
*225 g (8 oz) peas, fresh or frozen*
*225 g (8 oz) courgettes, cut into 2.5 cm (1-inch) batons*
*400 g can chopped tomatoes*
*40 g (1½ oz) creamed coconut*
*250 g (9 oz) egg noodles*
*1 pack of fresh coriander or basil, chopped roughly*
*salt and freshly ground black pepper*

1  Spray a large frying-pan or wok with low-fat cooking spray and put on a medium heat. Fry the onions until soft – about 4 minutes – and then add the monkfish and curry paste. Stir-fry for 2 minutes.
2  Add the beans, peas, courgettes, tomatoes, creamed coconut and seasonings. Add 300 ml (½ pint) water. Cook for 25 minutes, stirring occasionally.
3  While the curry is cooking, bring a large pan of water to the boil and cook the noodles as stated on the packet. Drain and keep warm.
4  Check the seasoning and add the chopped coriander or basil. Serve with the noodles.

**Monkfish and Coconut Curry with noodles: this deliciously fragrant curry is quick and easy to make, but great for both special occasions and family dinners.**

**Creamy Smoked Haddock Pasta:** a sunny yellow pasta dish with the flavours of kedgeree.

## CREAMY SMOKED HADDOCK PASTA

**POINTS**

per serving: 7          per recipe: 27½

*Serves 4*
*Preparation time: 5 minutes*
*Cooking time: 15 minutes*
*520 calories per serving*
*Freezing not recommended*

*350 g (12 oz) pasta shapes*
*2 x 175 g (6 oz) smoked haddock fillets*
*300 ml (½ pint) skimmed milk*
*a few strands of saffron (optional)*
*200 g (7 oz) low-fat soft cheese*
*40 g (1½ oz) raisins or sultanas*
*1 pack of fresh parsley, chopped*
*freshly ground black pepper*

1  Cook the pasta in plenty of salted boiling water, and then drain.

2  Meanwhile place the haddock fillets in a large pan, skin-side up and cover with the milk and saffron, if using. Bring to the boil and simmer gently for 5 minutes or until the fish is cooked.

3  Remove the fish from the milk with a fish slice. Gently flake it off the skin and into the cooked pasta. Stir the cheese, raisins and most of the parsley into the warm milk. Pour over the pasta and gently toss together.

4  Check the seasoning, add some pepper and sprinkle with the remaining chopped parsley.

## QUICK CREAMY PRAWN PASTA

**POINTS**

per serving: 7½          per recipe: 30

*Serves 4*
*Preparation time: 5 minutes*
*Cooking time: 5 minutes*
*465 calories per serving*
*Freezing not recommended*

A luscious sauce made with lots of garlic and finished with a dash of low-fat crème fraîche.

*350 g (12 oz) pasta*
*200 g (7 oz) tiger or king prawns, fresh or frozen and thawed*
*low-fat cooking spray*
*4 garlic cloves, chopped*
*200 g (7 oz) frozen peeled prawns, thawed*
*4 tablespoons sherry vinegar or dry sherry*
*150 ml (¼ pint) half-fat crème fraîche*
*1 pack of fresh parsley, chopped*
*salt and freshly ground black pepper*

1  Cook the pasta in plenty of salted boiling water.

2  Remove the heads and shells from the tiger or king prawns.

3  Spray a large frying-pan with the cooking spray and put on a medium heat. Add the garlic and fry until just turning golden. Add all the prawns, vinegar and seasoning and stir-fry for 4 minutes or until the large prawns are pink and cooked.

4  Remove from the heat and stir in the crème fraîche and fresh parsley.

5  Drain the pasta and toss with the prawn sauce. Check the seasoning and serve.

Californian
Salsa Salmon: a
light, fresh dish
packed full of
the sunshine
flavours of
California.

## CRAB AND GINGER NOODLES

**POINTS**

per serving: $4^{1}/_{2}$          per recipe: **18**

Serves 4
*Preparation time: 5 minutes*
*Cooking time: 10 minutes*
*350 calories per serving*
*Freezing not recommended*

250 g (9 oz) noodles
low-fat cooking spray
a bunch of spring onions
2.5 cm (1-inch) fresh ginger, peeled
and cut into thin slivers
2 garlic cloves, sliced
1 red chilli, de-seeded and chopped
finely (optional)
2 x 170 g canned crab meat
300 g ($10^{1}/_{2}$ oz) mange-tout or
sugar snaps
4 tablespoons soy sauce
1 pack of fresh coriander
1 tablespoon peanuts, chopped
and toasted

1  Cook the noodles in a large pan of salted boiling water as stated on the packet. Drain, rinse and drain again. Reserve.

2  Spray a large frying-pan or wok with the cooking spray and put on a high heat. Stir-fry the spring onions, ginger, garlic and chilli, if using, for a minute.

3  Add the crab, mange-tout or sugar snaps, noodles and soy sauce. Stir-fry for 2 minutes.

4  Take the wok off the heat, add the fresh coriander and serve sprinkled with peanuts.

## CALIFORNIAN SALSA SALMON

**POINTS**

per serving: $5^{1}/_{2}$          per recipe: **22**

Serves 4
*Preparation time: 10 minutes*
*Cooking time: 15 minutes*
*415 calories per serving*
*Freezing not recommended*

1 pack of fresh mint
2 x 175 g (6 oz) salmon fillets
240 g ($8^{1}/_{2}$ oz) pasta ribbons
FOR THE SALSA
250 g (9 oz) cherry tomatoes, halved
1 red onion, chopped finely
2 garlic cloves, chopped finely
$^{1}/_{2}$ cucumber, chopped finely
2 tablespoons capers, drained
and washed
1 red chilli, de-seeded and
chopped finely
juice and zest of 1 lime
(or 2 tablespoons lime juice)
1 teaspoon sugar
salt and freshly ground black pepper

1  Reserve a couple of sprigs of mint. Finely chop the rest.

2  Place the salmon fillets in a large pan, cover with water and add 1 sprig of mint. Bring to the boil and then turn off the heat, leaving the salmon to cook.

3  Meanwhile cook the pasta ribbons in plenty of salted, boiling water. Drain and return to the saucepan. Add all the salsa ingredients and the chopped mint, and toss together.

4  Drain the salmon and flake the flesh off the skin. Gently toss it with the pasta and serve garnished with the last sprig of mint.

VARIATION Fillets of rainbow trout would look and taste just as good in this recipe. Adjust the Points accordingly.

## SPICY SEAFOOD AND TOMATO PASTA

**POINTS**

per serving: 5½      per recipe: 22

*Serves 4*
*Preparation time: 5 minutes*
*Cooking time: 30 minutes*
*485 calories per serving*
*Freezing not recommended*

This seafood sauce can be cooked in a flash. If you're using fresh seafood, a mixture of prawns, mussels, squid and cockles is good.

350 g (12 oz) spaghetti
low-fat cooking spray
2 onions, chopped
2 garlic cloves, chopped finely
1 red chilli, de-seeded and chopped finely
400 g (14 oz) seafood selection, fresh or frozen and defrosted
2 tablespoons dry white wine
2 x 400 g cans chopped tomatoes
2 tablespoons Worcestershire sauce
1 teaspoon sugar or honey
1 pack of fresh basil, chopped
salt and freshly ground black pepper

1 Cook the pasta in plenty of salted, boiling water. Drain and keep warm.

2 Meanwhile, spray a large frying-pan or wok with the cooking spray and put it on a medium heat. Stir-fry the onions, garlic and chilli for 5 minutes or until the onions are soft.

3 Add the seafood, white wine, tomatoes, Worcestershire sauce, sugar or honey and seasoning and cook for 25 minutes or until the sauce is reduced and thick.

4 Check the seasoning and toss with the spaghetti. Sprinkle with chopped basil.

## SPAGHETTI WITH BABY CLAMS

**POINTS**

per serving: 5½      per recipe: 21½

*Serves 4*
*Preparation time: 5 minutes*
*Cooking time: 20 minutes*
*465 calories per serving*
*Freezing not recommended*

Clams, called 'vongole', are available in cans and jars, or you could use fresh mussels.

350 g (12 oz) spaghetti
low-fat cooking spray
2 onions, chopped
4 garlic cloves, chopped
150 ml (¼ pint) fish or vegetable stock
400 g can chopped tomatoes
1 teaspoon sugar
2 x 280 g cans baby clams, or fresh mussels (see Cook's tip)
2 teaspoons dried oregano or 1 pack of fresh parsley, chopped
salt and freshly ground black pepper

1 Cook the spaghetti in plenty of salted, boiling water. Drain, rinse and keep warm.

2 Meanwhile, spray a large frying-pan or wok with the cooking spray and put on a medium heat. Stir-fry the onions and garlic until softened and then add the stock, tomatoes, sugar and seasoning. Cook for 15 minutes or until reduced by a third.

3 Add the clams or mussels and the oregano or fresh parsley. As soon as the shellfish are heated through the sauce is ready. Pour over the spaghetti and serve immediately.

COOK'S TIP If you are using fresh mussels then first wash them under a running tap and remove the beards. Put them in a pan with the lid on and, giving them an occasional shake, cook for 4 minutes, or until most of the shells have opened. Throw away any that haven't opened. Remove the rest from their shells ready to add to the sauce.

**Spaghetti with Baby Clams: this makes a regular appearance on the menus of restaurants all over Italy.**

**Tagliatelle with Meatballs: perfect for the long winter evenings or any other time really!**

This chapter contains all your favourites like Bolognese and carbonara adapted to keep the Points lower without compromising on taste. There are also some more unusual recipes drawing on the cuisines of Morocco and the Orient. They are all easy to prepare and very satisfying.

## TAGLIATELLE WITH MEATBALLS

**POINTS**

per serving: 9½          per recipe: 39

*Serves 4*
*Preparation time: 30 minutes*
*Cooking time: 40 minutes*
*595 calories per serving*
*Freezing recommended*

This is a rich and satisfying dish. Save up some Points or earn a few Bonus Points in order to enjoy this special dish.

*low-fat cooking spray*

*240 g (8½ oz) tagliatelle*

*½ pack of fresh basil, chopped*

FOR THE MEATBALLS

*4 thick slices white bread, crusts removed and torn up*

*4 tablespoons skimmed milk*

*400 g (14 oz) extra-lean minced beef*

*2 garlic cloves, crushed*

*75 g (2¾ oz) mozzarella Light, chopped into small dice*

*1 egg, beaten*

*2 tablespoons Worcestershire sauce*

*½ pack of fresh basil, chopped*

*salt and freshly ground black pepper*

FOR THE SAUCE

*400 g can chopped tomatoes with herbs*

*200 ml (7 fl oz) beef stock*

*2 tablespoons sun-dried tomatoes, chopped finely (optional)*

*1 teaspoon sugar*

*salt and freshly ground black pepper*

1  Place the bread in a large bowl, add the milk and allow to soak for 5 minutes. Add all the other meatball ingredients and mix together. Roll small amounts in your hands to make about 20–24 meatballs.

2  Heat a large frying-pan and spray with low-fat cooking spray. Fry the meatballs in batches for 5 minutes to brown on all sides. Remove and drain on kitchen paper.

3  To make the sauce, drain any oil from the frying-pan and add the sauce ingredients. Bring to the boil and simmer for 20 minutes.

4  Meanwhile cook the tagliatelle in plenty of salted, boiling water. Drain and keep warm.

5  Add the meatballs to the sauce and simmer for a further 10 minutes, stirring occasionally. Check the seasoning and sprinkle with the basil before serving with the pasta.

## SPAGHETTI BOLOGNESE

**POINTS**

per serving: 6½          per recipe: 27

*Serves 4*
*Preparation time: 10 minutes*
*Cooking time: 50 minutes*
*490 calories per serving*
*Freezing recommended*

A 'normal', full-fat spaghetti bolognese is at least 11 Points a serving.

*low-fat cooking spray*
*2 onions, chopped finely*
*2 garlic cloves, chopped finely*
*400 g (14 oz) extra-lean minced beef*
*2 carrots, chopped finely*
*2 celery sticks, chopped finely*
*400 g (14 oz) can chopped tomatoes*
*2 tablespoons tomato purée*
*leaves from 2 sprigs of fresh thyme, or 1 teaspoon dried thyme*
*1 pack of fresh parsley, chopped or 2 teaspoons dried parsley*
*150 ml (¼ pint) red wine*
*2 tablespoons Worcestershire sauce*
*240 g (8½ oz) spaghetti*
*salt and freshly ground black pepper*

1 Spray a large frying-pan with cooking spray and put on a medium heat. Fry the onions and garlic until softened – about 4 minutes. Add the beef, breaking it up with the back of a wooden spoon to brown it all over.

2 Add the carrots, celery, tomatoes, tomato purée, thyme, dried parsley (if using – fresh waits until the end), seasoning, red wine and Worcestershire sauce. Stir and leave on a low heat to simmer for 45 minutes.

3 While the sauce is simmering, cook the spaghetti in plenty of salted, boiling water for 10 minutes.

4 Check the seasoning, stir in the fresh parsley, if using, and serve.

## SIZZLING BEEF NOODLES

**POINTS**

per serving: 7          per recipe: 28½

*Serves 4*
*Preparation time: 10 minutes + marinating time*
*Cooking time: 15 minutes*
*290 calories per serving*
*Freezing not recommended*

A colourful stir-fry bursting with flavour and nutrients.

*400 g (14 oz) rump steak, trimmed of fat and cut into thin strips*
FOR THE MARINADE
*2 garlic cloves, crushed*
*2 tablespoons soy sauce*
*2 tablespoons rice wine or dry sherry*
*2 tablespoons honey*
FOR THE STIR-FRY
*low-fat cooking spray*
*150 g (5½ oz) broccoli, cut into florets*
*2 red peppers, cut into strips*
*1 pack of spring onions, cut diagonally into 2.5 cm (1-inch) lengths*
*4 tablespoons teriyaki sauce*
*200 g pack of beansprouts*
*1 fresh chilli, de-seeded and sliced into thin strips, or 1 teaspoon dried chilli flakes*
*250 g (9 oz) noodles, cooked*
*salt and freshly ground black pepper*

1 Mix all the marinade ingredients together in a large bowl and add the beef. Allow to marinate for as long as possible up to 2 hours (though 5 minutes will do). Before cooking remove the beef from the marinade but reserve the juices.

2 Spray a large frying-pan or wok with the low-fat cooking spray, put on a high heat and stir-fry the beef. Put on a plate and keep warm.

3 Add the broccoli to the wok and 6 tablespoons of water. Stir-fry for 5 minutes. Add the peppers and spring onions and stir-fry for a further 3 minutes.

4 Stir in the teriyaki sauce and the remaining marinade. Return the beef to the wok, add the beansprouts, chilli or chilli flakes and the noodles. Stir-fry over a high heat for 2 minutes or until the beef is hot again. Check the seasoning and serve.

Spaghetti Bolognese: a lower fat version of this world famous sauce from Bologna, the rich city in Italy's north.

**Easy One Pot Lamb
Casserole: this is
a meltingly tender
hot pot best served
with pasta ribbons.**

## EASY ONE POT LAMB CASSEROLE

**POINTS**

per serving: 8½          per recipe: 35

Serves 4
Preparation time: 15 minutes
Cooking time: 2 hours
495 calories per serving
Freezing recommended

Gremolata is a garnish made of chopped herbs, lemon zest and garlic.

240 g (8½ oz) pasta ribbons

FOR THE CASSEROLE

2 tablespoons plain flour

8 medium loin lamb chops, trimmed of fat

low-fat cooking spray

1 onion, chopped finely

2 garlic cloves, chopped finely

1 carrot, chopped finely

1 celery stick, chopped finely

400 g can chopped tomatoes

150 ml (¼ pint) dry white wine

425 ml (¾ pint) lamb stock

salt and freshly ground black pepper

FOR THE GREMOLATA

1 pack of fresh mint, chopped finely

finely grated zest of 1 lemon

1 garlic clove, chopped finely

1  Preheat the oven to Gas Mark 3/160°C/325°F.

2  Mix together the flour and seasoning on a plate and dust the lamb chops in it. Spray a large frying-pan with low-fat cooking spray and brown the lamb on all sides. Place the lamb in a casserole.

3  Add all the other casserole ingredients and bake in the oven for 1¾–2 hours, turning the meat at half time.

4  Mix the gremolata ingredients together.

5  Cook the pasta ribbons in plenty of salted, boiling water.

6  Serve the meat with the noodles, sprinkled with the gremolata.

## MOROCCAN LAMB

**POINTS**

per serving: 8½          per recipe: 33½

Serves 4
Preparation time: 5 minutes
Cooking time: 2½ hours
520 calories per serving
Freezing recommended

This dish can be thrown together in minutes and then left on a slow simmer while you go and do something else.

410 g can prunes in prune juice

400 g (14 oz) minced lamb

½ teaspoon ground ginger

1 teaspoon ground coriander

2 teaspoons ground cinnamon

1 onion, chopped finely

1 tablespoon honey

240 g (8½ oz) spaghetti

salt and freshly ground black pepper

1  Drain the prunes, reserving the juice.

2  Place the meat in a large pan and cover with water and the prune juice. Add the ginger, seasoning, coriander, cinnamon and onion. Bring to the boil, cover the pan and simmer very gently for 2 hours.

3  Add the prunes and simmer for a further 20 minutes and then stir in the honey.

4  Meanwhile cook the spaghetti in plenty of salted, boiling water. Drain.

5  Serve the spaghetti topped with the sauce.

**Moroccan Lamb:** this is flavoured with the spices of Morocco and sweetened with prunes and honey.

## SPRING LAMB PASTA

**POINTS**

per serving: 7      per recipe: $28\frac{1}{2}$

*Serves 4*
*Preparation time: 10 minutes*
*Cooking time: 45 minutes*
*480 calories per serving*
*Freezing not recommended*

An easy supper dish that combines spring lamb with spring vegetables in a one-pot pasta meal. Use 'new season' lamb if possible.

175 g (6 oz) pasta
low-fat cooking spray
400 g (14 oz) lamb leg steaks, trimmed of fat and cubed
2 garlic cloves, chopped
leaves from 2 sprigs of rosemary
4 leeks, sliced
450 g (1 lb) carrots, sliced
175 g (6 oz) green beans
400 g can chopped tomatoes
500 ml (18 fl oz) lamb stock
125 g ($4\frac{1}{2}$ oz) mozzarella Light, sliced thinly
salt and freshly ground black pepper

1 Preheat the oven to Gas Mark 6/200°C/400°F.
2 Cook the pasta in plenty of boiling, salted water and then drain.
3 Spray a large frying-pan with low-fat cooking spray and put on a medium heat. Add the lamb, garlic, rosemary and seasoning. Brown the lamb all over.
4 Put the lamb in a casserole dish and add all the other ingredients, except the mozzarella, and mix well. Lay the mozzarella slices on top and bake in the hot oven for 40 minutes.

## SPAGHETTI CARBONARA

**POINTS**

per serving: 8      per recipe: 33

*Serves 4*
*Preparation time: 5 minutes*
*Cooking time: 15 minutes*
*530 calories per serving*
*Freezing not recommended*

This takes minutes to make with ingredients that are, hopefully, already in your fridge.

350 g (12 oz) spaghetti
low-fat cooking spray
8 rashers lean unsmoked, rindless back bacon, cut into small pieces
1 garlic clove, chopped finely
1 egg and 2 egg whites
100 g ($3\frac{1}{2}$ oz) low-fat soft cheese
1 pack of fresh parsley, chopped
salt and freshly ground black pepper

1 Cook the spaghetti in plenty of salted, boiling water for 10 minutes or until cooked and then drain.
2 Spray a large pan with low-fat cooking spray and put on a medium heat. Fry the bacon until crispy – about 5 minutes – then add the garlic and fry for a further minute.
3 Add the hot spaghetti to the bacon in the pan and quickly add the egg, egg whites, soft cheese, a little salt and lots of black pepper and toss together. The heat of the spaghetti should cook the eggs and very slightly thicken the sauce.
4 Stir in the fresh parsley and serve with more freshly ground black pepper.

## FRESH PEA AND HAM PASTA

**POINTS**

per serving: $5\frac{1}{2}$      per recipe: $22\frac{1}{2}$

*Serves 4*
*Preparation time: 5 minutes*
*Cooking time: 20 minutes*
*380 calories per serving*
*Freezing not recommended*

This sauce will bring back the flavours of summer all year round.

240 g ($8\frac{1}{2}$ oz) pasta shells
low-fat cooking spray
2 onions, chopped finely
300 g ($10\frac{1}{2}$ oz) frozen petit pois, defrosted
1 small lettuce, shredded
1 teaspoon sugar
200 g (7 oz) lean honey roast ham, cut into strips
4 tablespoons half-fat crème fraîche
1 pack of fresh mint, chopped
salt and freshly ground black pepper

1 Cook the pasta shells in plenty of boiling, salted water and then drain.
2 Meanwhile heat a large pan, spray with low-fat cooking spray and fry the onions until soft. Then add the peas, lettuce, sugar, seasoning and 2 tablespoons of water. Put a lid on the pan and cook for 10 minutes.
3 Stir in the ham, crème fraîche, mint and cooked pasta. Check the seasoning and serve.

**Spaghetti Carbonara: a low-fat version of the classic supper dish.**

**Sweet and Sour Pork Noodles: a substantial dish full of tempting flavours and vibrant colours that you can have on the table in minutes.**

## SWEET AND SOUR PORK NOODLES

**POINTS**

per serving: 6          per recipe: 25

*Serves 4*

*Preparation time: 5 minutes*

*Cooking time: 10 minutes*

*475 calories per serving*

*Freezing not recommended*

*400 g (14 oz) pork tenderloin, sliced thinly*

*1 teaspoon five-spice powder*

*2 tablespoons soy sauce*

*4 tablespoons cider vinegar*

*1 small pineapple or 397 g can pineapple in pineapple juice*

*250 g (9 oz) noodles*

*low-fat cooking spray*

*2 garlic cloves, sliced thinly*

*2.5 cm (1-inch) piece of fresh ginger, cut into matchsticks*

*1 orange pepper, cut into strips*

*1 green pepper cut into strips*

*1 teaspoon honey*

*1 tablespoon cornflour dissolved in 3 tablespoons water*

*a bunch of spring onions, chopped finely*

*salt and freshly ground black pepper*

1 Mix the pork with the five-spice powder, soy sauce and cider vinegar.

2 Peel the pineapple, if using. Cut the pineapple into chunks. Reserve the juice.

3 Cook the noodles.

4 Spray a wok or large frying-pan with the low-fat cooking spray and put it on a high heat. Add the pork, reserving the marinade. Add the garlic. Sear the pork on both sides.

5 Add the ginger, peppers and pineapple and stir-fry for 4 minutes or until the edges are browned.

6 Add the marinade, pineapple juice and honey and simmer for 2 minutes. Stir in the cornflour and water to thicken the sauce.

7 Check the seasoning. Sprinkle with the spring onions and serve with the hot noodles.

## GARLICKY PORK AND COURGETTE PASTA

**POINTS**

per serving: 6          per recipe: 24½

*Serves 4*

*Preparation time: 5 minutes*

*Cooking time: 15 minutes*

*505 calories per serving*

*Freezing not recommended*

This is a light, fresh-tasting pasta, perfect for lunch with friends or a late supper.

*400 g (14 oz) pork chops or cutlets*

*4 medium slices bread*

*250 g (9 oz) pasta*

*low-fat cooking spray*

*2 garlic cloves, chopped finely*

*450 g (1 lb) courgettes, cut into small dice*

*leaves from 4 sprigs of thyme*

*zest and juice of 1 lemon*

*2 tablespoons redcurrant jelly*

*150 ml (¼ pint) stock*

*salt and freshly ground black pepper*

1 Cut the pork off the bone and remove any fat. Chop the meat into small dice.

2 Process the bread in a food processor to make breadcrumbs. Toast the breadcrumbs under a hot grill.

3 Cook the pasta in plenty of salted, boiling water. Drain.

4 Meanwhile, spray a large frying-pan or wok with the low-fat cooking spray and put on a high heat. Fry the chopped garlic for 1 minute and then add the pork and some seasoning. Brown the meat all over about 4 minutes.

5 Add the courgettes, keeping the heat high, and stir-fry for another 2 minutes. Add the thyme, lemon juice (but not the zest), redcurrant jelly and stock. Boil rapidly for 2 minutes.

6 Add the cooked pasta to the pan and toss together. Check the seasoning.

7 Mix the breadcrumbs with the lemon zest. Serve the pasta with with the breadcrumb and lemon zest mixture sprinkled on top.

# SPICY SAUSAGE PASTA

| POINTS | |
| --- | --- |
| per serving: 6½ | per recipe: 26 |

*Serves 4*
*Preparation time: 5 minutes*
*Cooking time: 25 minutes*
*570 calories per serving*
*Freezing recommended*

*350 g (12 oz) pasta*
*low-fat cooking spray*
*454 g pack of 95% fat-free thick pork sausages, sliced*
*2 onions, sliced*
*2 garlic cloves, sliced*
*2 tablespoons dry white wine or water*
*6 sun-dried tomatoes, sliced*
*400 g can chopped tomatoes*
*1 red chilli, de-seeded and chopped finely or 1 teaspoon dried chilli flakes*
*¼ teaspoon ground nutmeg*
*½ teaspoon ground cloves*
*2 sprigs of fresh sage, chopped or 1 teaspoon dried sage + a little extra to garnish*
*300 ml (½ pint) stock*
*salt and freshly ground black pepper*

1 Cook the pasta in plenty of salted, boiling water and then drain.

2 Spray a large frying-pan with the cooking spray and put it on a medium heat. Brown the sausages all over. Add the onions and garlic and fry for 4 minutes or until softened.

3 Add the other ingredients and boil rapidly for 20 minutes or until the sauce is thick. Add the cooked pasta and toss together. Serve sprinkled with a little more fresh sage.

**Spicy Sausage Pasta: if you can find them, use spicy low-fat sausages.**

# CREAMY SAUSAGE & MUSTARD PASTA

| POINTS | |
| --- | --- |
| per serving: 6½ | per recipe: 26 |

*Serves 4*
*Preparation time: 5 minutes*
*Cooking time: 15 minutes*
*565 calories per serving*
*Freezing not recommended*

*350 g (12 oz) pasta ribbons*
*454 g pack of 99% fat-free thick pork sausages*
*1 garlic clove, chopped finely*
*250 g (9 oz) mushrooms, sliced*
*2 tablespoons Dijon mustard or wholegrain mustard*
*juice of 1 lemon*
*2 tablespoons half-fat crème fraîche*
*1 pack of fresh parsley, chopped*
*salt and freshly ground black pepper*

1 Cook the pasta in plenty of boiling, salted water for 15 minutes.

2 Remove the meat from the sausages.

3 Brown the sausagemeat in a large frying-pan. Add the garlic, mushrooms and seasoning.

4 When the mushrooms are cooked, add the mustard, lemon juice and 2 tablespoons of water.

5 Remove from the heat and stir in the crème fraîche. Check the seasoning. Serve with the pasta and serve sprinkled with parsley.

Creamy Sausage and Mustard Pasta: the ultimate comfort food that takes minutes to make.

**Chicken and Ricotta Parcels: this is a dish with gutsy flavours.**

# poultry

Chicken and turkey are perfect for the healthy Weight Watchers Programme. This chapter contains quick, tasty stir frys, one pot casseroles and a wonderful turkey cannelloni to tempt your tastebuds without affecting your waistline.

## CHICKEN AND RICOTTA PARCELS

**POINTS**

per serving: $8^1/_2$    per recipe: $33^1/_2$

*Serves 4*
*Preparation time: 10 minutes*
*Cooking time: 15 minutes*
*515 calories per serving*
*Freezing not recommended*

Serve with grilled or roasted vegetables or salad – don't forget to count the extra Points. You will need some cocktail sticks for this recipe.

*100 g (3½ oz) ricotta cheese*
*2 sprigs of fresh rosemary or sage, chopped, or 1 teaspoon dried rosemary or sage*
*1 shallot, chopped finely*
*4 medium skinless, boneless chicken breasts*
*2 tablespoons honey*
*1 teaspoon chilli powder or cayenne pepper*
*350 g (12 oz) plain ribbon pasta*
*salt and freshly ground black pepper*

1  In a bowl mix the ricotta cheese with the chopped herbs, shallot and freshly ground black pepper.

2  Cut a deep slit in the side of the chicken breasts and open out to form a pocket. Stuff each breast with a spoonful of the cheese mixture. Secure the pocket with a cocktail stick. Place the chicken breasts on a grill pan.

3  In a small pan mix the honey and chilli or cayenne. Melt the honey a little if it is not already runny. Brush the chicken with the honey mixture and place under a hot grill for 7–8 minutes, until golden brown. Then turn over, brush the other side and grill for another 7–8 minutes or until cooked through.

4  Cook the pasta in plenty of salted boiling water.

5  Remove the cocktail sticks before serving the chicken with the pasta.

## CARIBBEAN CHICKEN PASTA

**POINTS**

per serving: $7^1/_2$    per recipe: $31$

*Serves 4*
*Preparation time: 10 minutes*
*Cooking time: 20 minutes*
*520 calories per serving*
*Freezing not recommended*

For this sunshine-filled dish, spicy chicken fillets are paired with a cool, refreshing salsa.

*4 medium chicken breast fillets*
*350 g (12 oz) pasta*
FOR THE MARINADE
*4 tablespoons reduced-sugar lemon and lime marmalade*
*1 red chilli, de-seeded and chopped finely, or 1 teaspoon dried chilli flakes*
*2 tablespoons teriyaki sauce*
FOR THE SALSA
*250 g (9 oz) cherry tomatoes, halved*
*1 red onion, chopped finely*
*½ cucumber, chopped finely*
*1 green pepper, de-seeded and chopped finely*
*zest and juice of 2 limes*
*2 teaspoons sugar*
*salt and freshly ground black pepper*

1  Preheat the oven to Gas Mark 5/190°C/375°F.

2  Mix the marinade ingredients together in a small pan and heat, stirring, until combined.

3  Place the chicken fillets in an ovenproof dish and pour the marinade over. Cover with foil and bake in the oven for 10 minutes. Then baste the chicken and remove the foil. Cook for another 10 minutes, or until cooked through.

4  Meanwhile, cook the pasta in plenty of salted, boiling water. Drain.

5  Combine all the salsa ingredients.

6  Slice the chicken into thick pieces.

7  Toss the chicken and the marinade into the warm pasta. Add the salsa and toss again. Check the seasoning.

## CHICKEN CACCIATORE

### POINTS

| per serving: 8½ | per recipe: 33½ |
|---|---|

Serves 4
Preparation time: 10 minutes
Cooking time: 45 minutes
585 calories per serving
Freezing recommended

low-fat cooking spray

450 g (1 lb) chicken pieces, skinless but on the bone

4 rashers lean, back bacon

2 onions, sliced finely

2 garlic cloves, sliced finely

150 ml (¼ pint) dry white wine

2 x 400 g cans chopped tomatoes

1 bay leaf

1 pack of fresh oregano or 2 teaspoons dried oregano

225 g (8 oz) button mushrooms

1 teaspoon sugar

240 g (8½ oz) pasta ribbons

salt and freshly ground black pepper

1  Spray a large pan with the low-fat cooking spray and put on a high heat. Brown the chicken pieces on all sides and season. Remove to a plate.

2  Add the bacon, onions and garlic to the pan, turn down the heat and stir-fry for 4 minutes or until the onions have started to soften.

3  Pour in the wine and cook on a high heat for 2 minutes, scraping up the sediment from the bottom of the pan. Add the tomatoes, bay leaf, oregano, mushrooms and seasoning, including the sugar, and simmer, covered with a lid, for 15 minutes.

4  Uncover and simmer for a further 20 minutes or until the sauce is thick.

5  Meanwhile cook the pasta in plenty of boiling, salted water and drain. Serve with the sauce.

WEIGHT WATCHERS TIP Water could be used instead of the dry white wine. Points per serving will be the same.

## LEMON CHICKEN PASTA

### POINTS

| per serving: 7 | per recipe: 28½ |
|---|---|

Serves 4
Preparation time: 10 minutes
Cooking time: 50 minutes
530 calories per serving
Freezing not recommended

Chicken breasts are roasted with lemon, garlic and rosemary and tossed with pasta to make this robust country-style dish.

4 teaspoons whole-grain mustard

2 tablespoons honey

4 medium chicken breasts, preferably on the bone, but skinless

1 garlic bulb, broken into cloves but not peeled

4 red onions, cut into 8 wedges

leaves from 4 sprigs of rosemary

1 lemon, quartered

300 ml (½ pint) chicken stock

350 g (12 oz) pasta

salt and freshly ground black pepper

1  Preheat the oven to Gas Mark 6/200°C/400°F.

2  Mix together the mustard and honey and spread on top of each chicken breast. Place the breasts in a deep baking tray with the garlic cloves, onion wedges and rosemary leaves. Squeeze over the lemon juice and place the leftover lemon peel in the tray too.

3  Pour over the stock and season.

4  Cover with foil and place in the oven for 45 minutes. Then remove the foil and cook for a further 5 minutes.

5  Meanwhile cook the pasta in plenty of salted, boiling water and drain.

6  Remove the lemon peel and the chicken breasts from the oven tray Toss the cooked pasta in with the vegetables and juices in the tray. Serve each portion of pasta topped with a sliced chicken breast.

Chicken Cacciatore: a vibrant, richly flavoured chicken stew to serve with plain pasta ribbons.

**Summer Chicken Casserole:** this one-pot meal is simplicity itself to make.

## SUMMER CHICKEN CASEROLLE

**POINTS**

| per serving: 9½ | per recipe: 37½ |
|---|---|

*Serves 4*
*Preparation time: 10 minutes*
*Cooking time: 1 hour*
*720 calories per serving*
*Freezing not recommended*

This is elegant enough, served with plain ribbon pasta, to serve up at a dinner party.

*low-fat cooking spray*
*450 g (1 lb) skinless chicken pieces*
*2 garlic cloves, sliced*
*12 baby onions or small shallots*
*150 ml (¼ pint) dry white wine*
*1 litre (1¾ pints) chicken or vegetable stock*
*8 baby carrots, scrubbed*
*8 baby turnips, scrubbed and halved*
*8 baby parsnips, scrubbed (450 g/1 lb)*
*200 g (7 oz) frozen or fresh peas*
*350 g (12 oz) pasta ribbons*
*4 tablespoons half-fat crème fraîche*
*salt and freshly ground black pepper*

1 Spray a large casserole or saucepan with low-fat cooking spray and put on a medium heat. Brown the chicken on all sides, season and remove to a plate.

2 Put the garlic and onions or shallots in the pan and fry until softened and golden – about 4 minutes – over a medium heat. Then add the wine and scrape the bottom of the pan with a wooden spoon for 1 minute.

3 Return the chicken to the pan and add the stock. Bring to the boil and then simmer for 45 minutes.

4 Add the vegetables to the pan and simmer for a further 15 minutes.

5 Cook the pasta ribbons in plenty of salted, boiling water. Drain.

6 Stir the crème fraîche into the casserole and check the seasoning before serving with the noodles.

## CREAMY CHICKEN LIVER PASTA

**POINTS**

| per serving: 6½ | per recipe: 26½ |
|---|---|

*Serves 4*
*Preparation time: 5 minutes*
*Cooking time: 15 minutes*
*435 calories per serving*
*Freezing not recommended*

*350 g (12 oz) spaghetti*
*300 g (10½ oz) chicken livers, fresh or frozen and defrosted*
*low-fat cooking spray*
*1 onion, sliced*
*4 bay leaves*
*1 teaspoon nutmeg*
*3 tablespoons dry sherry*
*2 tablespoons tomato purée*
*2 tablespoons half-fat crème fraîche*
*salt and freshly ground black pepper*

1 Cook the pasta in plenty of salted, boiling water. Drain.

2 Meanwhile cut the chicken livers into small slivers. Spray a large frying-pan with the low-fat cooking spray and put on a medium heat. Fry the onion until soft – about 4 minutes – and then add the chicken livers, bay leaves and seasoning. Fry for another 6 minutes over a low heat.

3 Turn up the heat and add the nutmeg and sherry. Let the alcohol evaporate for 1–2 minutes and then stir in the tomato purée, crème fraîche and 2 tablespoons of water.

4 Remove the bay leaves, check the seasoning and toss the pasta in the sauce to serve.

**Creamy Chicken Liver Pasta: this is a light version of this classic, smooth sauce.**

## QUICK DUCK NOODLES

**POINTS**

per serving: 5½          per recipe: 21½

*Serves 4*
*Preparation time: 5 minutes*
*Cooking time: 10 minutes*
*405 calories per serving*
*Freezing not recommended*

*2 boneless duck breasts, about 175 g*
*(6 oz) each, skinned and cut into strips*
*1 teaspoon Chinese five-spice powder*
*2 tablespoons soy sauce*
*2 teaspoons honey*

*250 g (9 oz) noodles*
*low-fat cooking spray*
*1 garlic clove, chopped finely*
*2.5 cm (1-inch) piece root ginger,*
*peeled and chopped finely*
*a bunch of spring onions, cut into*
*2.5 cm (1-inch) lengths*
*220 g can water chestnuts, drained*
*220 g can bamboo shoots, drained*
*300 g (10½ oz) fresh beansprouts*
*150 g (5½ oz) baby spinach or*
*watercress*
*juice and zest of 2 large oranges*
*1 tablespoon cornflour mixed with*
*2 tablespoons water*
*1 pack of fresh coriander, chopped*
*(optional)*

1 Combine the duck with the Chinese five-spice, soy sauce and honey in a bowl.

2 Cook noodles as stated on the packet.

3 Spray a large frying-pan or wok with the low-fat cooking spray and put on a high heat. Stir-fry the garlic, ginger and spring onions for 2 minutes. Add the duck and any juices. Stir-fry for another 2 minutes.

4 Add the water chestnuts, bamboo shoots, beansprouts, spinach or watercress, noodles and the orange juice. Cook for a further 4 minutes.

5 Stir in the cornflour mixture until the sauce thickens.

6 Serve sprinkled with the orange zest and fresh coriander, if using.

## MEDITERRANEAN TURKEY PASTA

**POINTS**

per serving: 7½          per recipe: 30½

*Serves 4*
*Preparation time: 15 minutes*
*Cooking time: 45 minutes*
*620 calories per serving*
*Freezing not recommended*

The Mediterranean flavours of tomatoes, peppers, aubergines and oregano liven up grilled turkey escalopes to make a perfect *al fresco* lunch dish served hot or cold.

*2 aubergines, cut into 1 cm (½-inch)*
*cubes*
*2 red peppers, de-seeded and cut into*
*1 cm (½-inch) pieces*
*2 orange peppers, de-seeded and cut*
*into 1 cm (½-inch) pieces*
*2 yellow peppers, de-seeded and cut*
*into 1 cm (½-inch) pieces*
*4 garlic cloves, sliced*
*8 tomatoes, quartered*
*4 teaspoons dried oregano or 2*
*teaspoons dried plus 1 pack of fresh*
*oregano, chopped*
*low-fat cooking spray*
*2 tablespoons plain flour*
*4 tablespoons dried breadcrumbs*
*2 egg whites*
*4 turkey escalopes, each weighing*
*about 115 g (4 oz)*
*350 g (12 oz) pasta shapes*
*1 pack of fresh basil, torn up*
*salt and freshly ground black pepper*

1 Preheat the oven to Gas Mark 6/200°C/400°F. Place the aubergines, peppers, garlic and tomatoes on a large ovenproof tray. Sprinkle with 2 teaspoons dried oregano or the chopped fresh oregano and some seasoning. Spray with the cooking spray and bake for 40 minutes, stirring occasionally.

2 Meanwhile put the flour on a plate and season. Put the breadcrumbs on another plate and add 2 teaspoons of dried oregano. Beat the egg whites in a shallow dish.

3 15 minutes before the baking time is up dip the turkey escalopes in the seasoned flour, and then in the egg white and then the breadcrumbs and oregano. Place them under a hot grill for 7–9 minutes. Turn them over for another 7–9 minutes to cook through.

4 Cook the pasta in plenty of boiling, salted water. Drain.

5 Slice the hot turkey and toss together with the pasta, roasted vegetables and fresh basil. Check the seasoning and serve.

**Quick Duck Noodles: this fragrant dish combines Chinese five-spice powder with orange for a quick treat.**

**Turkey Cannelloni:** this is a low-fat version of a very satisfying and tasty dish.

# PERSIAN TURKEY PASTA

**POINTS**

per serving: 7      per recipe: 28½

Serves 4

Preparation time: 10 minutes + marinating

Cooking time: 15 minutes

565 calories per serving

Freezing not recommended

Strips of turkey are baked with low-fat plain yogurt, spices and apricots and a sprinkling of toasted almonds for a delicious, light supper dish.

| |
|---|
| 350 g (12 oz) turkey stir-fry strips |
| 450 g (1 lb) low-fat plain yogurt |
| 2 teaspoons ground cumin |
| 1 teaspoon cinnamon |
| 1 teaspoon cayenne pepper |
| 150 g (5½ oz) dried apricots, chopped |
| 350 g (12 oz) pasta shapes |
| 25 g (1 oz) flaked almonds |
| juice of ½ lemon |
| 1 pack of fresh mint, chopped (optional) |
| salt and freshly ground black pepper |

1  In a bowl mix the turkey strips with the yogurt, spices, apricots and seasoning. Leave in the fridge for as long as possible (10 minutes is OK, overnight is better).

2  Preheat the oven to Gas Mark 9/240°C/475°F.

3  Cook the pasta in plenty of salted, boiling water for 10–15 minutes. Drain and keep warm.

4  Place the turkey and the marinade on a deep baking tray and bake for 15 minutes. Remove from the oven and pour off any juices in the tray. Reserve the juices.

5  Heat the grill and toast the flaked almonds.

6  In a large bowl toss together the turkey, its juices, the almonds and pasta. Add some seasoning and lemon juice to taste. Sprinkle with chopped mint, if using, and serve.

# TURKEY CANNELLONI

**POINTS**

per serving: 7½      per recipe: 29½

Serves 4

Preparation time: 20 minutes

Cooking time: 1 hour

485 calories per serving

Freezing not recommended

Buy the cannelloni which doesn't need any precooking.

| |
|---|
| 250 g (9 oz) no-precook cannelloni tubes |
| 1 pack of fresh parsley, chopped |
| 2 teaspoons paprika |
| salt and freshly ground black pepper |
| FOR THE FILLING |
| 15 g (½ oz) dried porcini mushrooms |
| low-fat cooking spray |
| 450 g (1 lb) turkey mince |
| 2 onions, diced finely |
| 4 garlic cloves, crushed |
| leaves from 4 sprigs of fresh thyme or 2 teaspoons dried thyme |
| 1 tablespoon Worcestershire sauce |
| FOR THE TOPPING |
| 2 teaspoons cornflour mixed with 1 tablespoon water |
| 450 g (1 lb) very low-fat plain yogurt |
| 100 g (3½ oz) low-fat soft cheese |

1  Preheat the oven to Gas Mark 6/200°C/400°F.

2  If using porcini mushrooms soak them in 150 ml (¼ pint) boiling water for 20 minutes. Then chop them, reserving the soaking liquid.

3  Make the filling. Spray a large frying-pan with the cooking spray and put it on a medium heat. Add the turkey mince, onions and garlic and some seasoning. Fry until the mince is browned all over. Add the porcini mushrooms and their soaking liquid, the thyme and Worcestershire sauce. Cook for 15 minutes or until most of the liquid has evaporated.

4  Fill the cannelloni tubes with spoonfuls of this mixture and lay in a large ovenproof dish.

5  Make the topping by mixing the cornflour paste into the yogurt to stabilise it. Then add the soft cheese and seasoning. Pour over the cannelloni.

6  Bake in the oven for 45 minutes.

7  Before serving sprinkle with fresh chopped parsley and paprika.

COOK'S NOTE Porcini mushrooms are strongly flavoured Italian mushrooms that can be bought dried. Soak them in enough boiling water to cover them for 20–30 minutes. Use the soaking liquid as well as the mushrooms.

**Fresh Tomato Pasta:** this is best made when tomatoes are good and ripe and with lots of fresh basil or parsley.

Our awareness of vegetarian food has increased enormously over the last decade. It is now seen as an exciting cuisine in its own right and as a healthy option that can be included in all our diets. These recipes include old favourites like a vegetarian lasagne but also some new, different combinations like cauliflower baked with spices and a beetroot and crème fraîche pasta sauce.

## FRESH TOMATO PASTA

**POINTS**

per serving: 4      per recipe: 17

Ⓥ Serves 4

*Preparation time: 5 minutes*
*Cooking time: 15 minutes*
*375 calories per serving*

This is the opposite of a long, slow-cooked pasta sauce. It is hardly cooked at all. It makes an excellent pizza topping.

*350 g (12 oz) pasta*
*low-fat cooking spray*
*1 onion, chopped roughly*
*2 garlic cloves, crushed*
*1 kg (2 lb 4 oz) ripe tomatoes, chopped roughly*
*1 pack of fresh basil or parsley, chopped*
*salt and freshly ground black pepper*

1 Cook the pasta in plenty of salted, boiling water. Drain.

2 Spray a large frying-pan with cooking spray and put on a medium heat. Stir-fry the onion and garlic until soft – about 4 minutes – and then add the tomatoes. Season. Cook for about 15 minutes on a medium heat or until the tomatoes have broken down.

3 Toss the pasta into the sauce with the fresh basil or parsley, and serve.

## GRILLED VEGETABLE PASTA

**POINTS**

per serving: 4½      per recipe: 19

Ⓥ Serves 4

*Preparation time: 10 minutes*
*Cooking time: 30 minutes*
*425 calories per serving*
*Freezing not recommended*

This dish brings together the smokey flavour of char-grilled vegetables with mint and balsamic vinegar. This dish is also very good cold. This gives time for the flavours to combine and mellow.

*350 g (12 oz) pasta*
*2 red onions, cut into 8 wedges*
*225 g (8 oz) courgettes, cut diagonally into 1 cm (½-inch) slices*
*225 g (8 oz) carrots, cut diagonally into 1 cm (½-inch) slices*
*2 red peppers, de-seeded and cut into 1 cm (½-inch) strips*
*1 bulb fennel, cut into 1 cm (½-inch) slices*
*1 bulb garlic, split into cloves but not peeled*
*low-fat cooking spray*
FOR THE DRESSING
*2 tablespoons balsamic vinegar*
*2 teaspoons olive oil*
*1 pack of fresh mint, chopped*
*salt and freshly ground black pepper*

1 Preheat the oven to Gas Mark 6/200°C/400°.

2 Cook the pasta in plenty of salted, boiling water. Drain and keep warm.

3 Meanwhile, lay the vegetables and garlic in the largest roasting tin you have, preferably so they create only one layer. Spray the vegetables with the low-fat cooking spray and toss together. Season them and roast in the oven for 40 minutes or until the edges have begun to blacken.

4 Toss the pasta in the roasting tin with the vegetables and the dressing ingredients.

WEIGHT WATCHERS NOTE Serve with thin shavings of parmesan if your Points allow. 3–4 shavings of parmesan (15 g/½ oz) is 1½ Points or 15 calories.

## CREAMY ASPARAGUS PASTA

**POINTS**

| per serving: 5 | per recipe: 20 |
|---|---|

Ⓥ Serves 4

*Preparation time: 5 minutes*
*Cooking time: 10 minutes*
*370 calories per serving*
*Freezing not recommended*

**Easy Mushroom Pasta: mushrooms are a traditional partner for pasta.**

350 g (12 oz) pasta
450 g (1 lb) asparagus, woody bases removed, cut into 2.5 cm (1-inch) lengths
2 tablespoons low-fat fromage frais
juice and zest of 1 lemon
4 tablespoons toasted breadcrumbs
salt and freshly ground black pepper

1 Cook the pasta in plenty of boiling, salted water. Steam the asparagus or cook it in an inch of boiling water for 4 minutes in a pan with a lid on.
2 Drain the pasta and mix with the asparagus, fromage frais, lemon juice and seasoning.
3 Mix the toasted breadcrumbs with the lemon zest and sprinkle over the top of the pasta before serving.

## EASY MUSHROOM PASTA

**POINTS**

| per serving: 4 | per recipe: 17 |
|---|---|

Ⓥ Serves 4

*Preparation time: 5 minutes*
*Cooking time: 10 minutes*
*345 calories per serving*
*Freezing not recommended*

350 g (12 oz) pasta
low-fat cooking spray
2 garlic cloves, chopped
450 g (1 lb) mushrooms, chopped
juice of 1 lemon
1 pack of chives, snipped
salt and freshly ground black pepper

1 Cook the pasta in plenty of salted, boiling water. Drain.
2 Meanwhile, spray a frying-pan with low-fat cooking spray and put on a medium heat. Fry the garlic until just turning golden then add the mushrooms and cook over a high heat for 4 minutes. Squeeze over the lemon juice and season.
3 Toss the pasta with the mushrooms and the chives and serve.

## PASTA PRIMAVERA

**POINTS**

| per serving: 5 | per recipe: 19½ |
|---|---|

Ⓥ Serves 4

*Preparation time: 5 minutes*
*Cooking time: 10 minutes*
*420 calories per serving*
*Freezing not recommended*

350 g (12 oz) pasta
low-fat cooking spray
200 g (7 oz) asparagus, cut into 2.5 cm (1-inch) lengths
300 g (10½ oz) sugar snap peas
300 g (10½ oz) baby carrots, trimmed
2 tablespoons dry white wine
100 g (3½ oz) low-fat soft cheese
1 pack of fresh dill, chopped
salt and freshly ground black pepper

1 Cook the pasta in plenty of boiling salted water. Drain.
2 Spray a large saucepan or wok with the low-fat cooking spray and put it on a medium heat. Stir-fry all the vegetables with the white wine for 4 minutes.
3 Add the soft cheese and gently stir in. Season and toss with the pasta and fresh dill.

**Pasta Primavera: primavera is the Italian word for spring.**

**Creamy Asparagus Pasta: this simple sauce does not detract from the fabulous flavour of the asparagus.**

# BRIGHT BEETROOT SAUCE

**V** Serves 4

*Preparation time: 5 minutes*

*Cooking time: 10 minutes*

*405 calories per serving*

*Freezing not recommended*

*350 g (12 oz) pasta*

*6 medium-sized beetroot, cooked, peeled and cubed*

*100 ml (3½ fl oz) half-fat crème fraîche*

*1 pack of fresh parsley, dill or basil, chopped*

*salt and freshly ground black pepper*

1 Cook the pasta in plenty of boiling, salted water. Drain.

2 Toss the pasta with the other ingredients and serve.

---

**Bright Beetroot Sauce: for fans of delicious beetroot this fantastically coloured pasta is a fragrant summer treat.**

# VEGETABLE LASAGNE

**V** Serves 4

*Preparation time: 5 minutes*

*Cooking time: 35 minutes*

*485 calories per serving*

*Freezing not recommended*

Using the ready-prepared jars of ragu this substantial and nutritious dish can be out of the oven to feed a hungry family in very little time.

*250 g (9 oz) no-precook lasagne sheets, preferably spinach*

FOR THE FILLING

*225 g (8 oz) mushrooms, chopped roughly*

*225 g (8 oz) frozen mixed vegetables, defrosted*

*225 g (8 oz) broccoli, cut into small florets*

*455 g jar low-fat ragu sauce*

FOR THE TOPPING

*2 eggs*

*4 tablespoons skimmed milk*

*300 g (10½ oz) low-fat plain yogurt*

*100 g (3½ oz ) low-fat soft cheese*

*4 teaspoons parmesan cheese*

*salt and freshly ground black pepper*

1 Preheat the oven to Gas Mark 5/190°C/375°F.

2 Place all the filling ingredients together in a saucepan, cover and bring to the boil. Then remove the lid and simmer for 10 minutes.

3 Put a layer of vegetables in an ovenproof dish. Top with a layer of lasagne. Repeat with layers of vegetables and lasagne until the vegetables are used up.

4 In a bowl beat the eggs and milk. Add the yogurt and soft cheese and some seasoning. Pour this over the lasagne and sprinkle with the parmesan. Bake in the oven for 25 minutes.

## SPICED CAULIFLOWER PASTA

**POINTS**

per serving: **5**          per recipe: **20**

V *Serves 4*
*Preparation time: 5 minutes*
*Cooking time: 20 minutes*
*395 calories per serving*
*Freezing not recommended*

This is a very unusual way to cook cauliflower, but once you've tried it I guarantee you'll try it again and again.

*1 large cauliflower, cut into florets*
*2 tablespoons ground cumin*
*1 tablespoon ground cinnamon*
*350 g (12 oz) pasta*
*300 g (10½ oz) low-fat plain yogurt*
*1 pack of fresh coriander or mint*
*salt and freshly ground black pepper*

1 Preheat the oven to Gas Mark 8/230°C/450°F. Toss the cauliflower florets in the cumin and cinnamon in a baking tray and roast in the oven for 20 minutes or until softened and slightly charred.

2 Meanwhile cook the pasta in plenty of salted, boiling water. Drain.

3 Toss the pasta into the cooked cauliflower and stir in the yogurt, coriander or mint and seasoning.

## WINTER VEGETABLE PASTA

**POINTS**

per serving: **6**          per recipe: **23½**

V *Serves 4*
*Preparation time: 10 minutes*
*Cooking time: 45 minutes–1 hour*
*515 calories per serving*
*Freezing not recommended*

Winter vegetables are cooked until meltingly soft and then tossed with low-fat soft cheese to make a comforting, warming pasta for winter nights.

*6 carrots*
*4 medium parsnips*
*2 onions*
*1 small pumpkin or squash*
*450 g (1 lb) Brussels sprouts, halved*
*8 unpeeled garlic cloves, smashed*
*leaves from 4 sprigs of rosemary or*
*2 teaspoons dried rosemary*
*low-fat cooking spray*
*350 g (12 oz) pasta*
*100 g (3½ oz) low-fat soft cheese*
*salt and freshly ground black pepper*

1 Preheat oven to Gas Mark 6/200°C/400°F.

2 Cut the carrots and parsnips into quarters or sixths lengthways, depending on their size. Cut the onions into eighths. Peel the pumpkin or squash and cut into bite-sized pieces.

3 Put all the vegetables and garlic in a large roasting tin, season, sprinkle over the rosemary and spray with the cooking spray. Roast in the oven for 45 minutes–1 hour or until the vegetables are soft.

4 Ten to fifteen minutes before the end of the roasting time, cook the pasta in plenty of salted, boiling water. Drain.

5 Toss the vegetables with the pasta in the roasting tin and stir in the soft cheese. Check the seasoning and serve.

## ROASTED TOMATO PASTA

**POINTS**

per serving: 7½      per recipe: 30

Ⓥ Serves 4
Preparation time: 5 minutes
Cooking time: 30 minutes
530 calories per serving
Freezing not recommended

Plum tomatoes roast well because their flesh is dense and they are not very juicy.

1 kg (2 lb 4 oz) plum tomatoes
200 g (7 oz) dried breadcrumbs
2 garlic cloves, crushed
1 pack of parsley or basil, chopped
75 g (2¾ oz) currants
8 anchovies, rinsed and chopped
350 g (12 oz) pasta ribbons

1 Preheat the oven to Gas Mark 6/200°C/400°F.
2 Cut the tomatoes in half around their circumference. Push out most of the seeds with your finger or a spoon. Stand the tomatoes up in a large roasting tin.
3 Mix the breadcrumbs, garlic, parsley or basil, currants and anchovies together in a bowl. Put a teaspoon of the mixture into each tomato. Roast in the oven for 30 minutes.
4 Meanwhile cook the pasta in plenty of boiling, salted water. Drain. Serve with the tomatoes.

## BAKED AUBERGINE PASTA

**POINTS**

per serving: 4½      per recipe: 19

Ⓥ Serves 4
Preparation time: 5 minutes
Cooking time: 40 minutes
365 calories per serving
Freezing not recommended

In this recipe aubergines are baked slowly and then mixed with low-fat crème fraîche and garlic to make the most wonderful, soothing pasta sauce.

2 aubergines
4 unpeeled garlic cloves
350 g (12 oz) pasta
4 tablespoons half-fat crème fraîche
juice of ½ lemon
1 pack of fresh basil or parsley, chopped
salt and freshly ground black pepper

1 Preheat the oven to Gas Mark 6/200°C/400°F. Place the aubergines and the garlic on a roasting tray and bake for 40 minutes, turning once.
2 Meanwhile cook the pasta in plenty of salted, boiling water. Drain.
3 When the aubergines are cooked, cut them in half lengthways and spoon out the soft flesh into a bowl. Pop the garlic out of its skin and add to the aubergine. Add the crème fraîche, lemon juice and seasoning and mash everything together.
4 Toss the pasta in the sauce and sprinkle with fresh basil or parsley.

## PASTA RATATOUILLE

**POINTS**

per serving: 4½      per recipe: 17½

Ⓥ Serves 4
Preparation time: 5 minutes
Cooking time: 50 minutes
400 calories per serving
Freezing not recommended

This classic sauce from France is perfect with pasta and low in Points too.

350 g (12 oz) pasta
1 pack of fresh basil, chopped (optional)
FOR THE RATATOUILLE
low-fat cooking spray
2 onions, chopped roughly
2 garlic cloves, chopped roughly
1 large aubergine, cubed roughly
4 courgettes, sliced
2 green peppers, de-seeded and sliced
400 g can chopped tomatoes with herbs
leaves from 3 sprigs of fresh thyme or rosemary or 1 teaspoon dried thyme or rosemary
1 teaspoon sugar
salt and freshly ground pepper

1 Spray a large pan with the cooking spray and put on a medium heat. Add the onions and garlic and cook for 4 minutes, until softened.
2 Add the other ratatouille ingredients, some seasoning and the sugar. Simmer for 45 minutes or until reduced and thickened.
3 Meanwhile cook the pasta in plenty of boiling, salted water then drain.
4 Check the seasoning of the sauce, toss with the pasta and serve with fresh basil, if using.

**Roasted Tomato Pasta: this recipe takes very little effort to prepare and the full, intense flavour makes the wait worthwhile.**

**Mushroom and Sweet Onion Pasta: onions and mushrooms are cooked until they are meltingly sweet and soft in this simply delicious recipe.**

# super quick & easy pasta

These are the easiest of easy sauces, the quickest of the quick. They're for when you want some food and you want it NOW. No need to resort to convenience snacks, just get that water boiling. These recipes enable you to get a meal on the table in record time with ingredients that you may already have in your store-cupboard or fridge. Bread and a simple side salad are optional extras – just remember to count any extra Points.

## MUSHROOM AND SWEET ONION PASTA

**POINTS**

per serving: 4        per recipe: 17

 *Serves 4*

*Preparation time: 5 minutes*
*Cooking time: 20 minutes*
*365 calories per serving*
*Freezing not recommended*

---

*350 g (12 oz) pasta*

*low-fat cooking spray*

*250 g (9 oz) mushrooms, sliced*

*4 onions, sliced finely*

*300 ml (½ pint) vegetable stock*

*leaves from 4 sprigs of fresh thyme,*
*2 teaspoons dried thyme*

*salt and freshly ground pepper*

1 Cook the pasta in plenty of boiling, salted water. Drain.

2 Meanwhile, spray a large frying-pan with the cooking spray and put on a high heat. Stir-fry the mushrooms and onions until they are golden brown. Add the stock and thyme and turn the heat down to a simmer.

3 Simmer until most of the stock has evaporated and the onions are soft – about 15 minutes. Check the seasoning and toss with the pasta.

## FIERY GARLIC PASTA

### POINTS
per serving: 5½          per recipe: 21½

Ⓥ Serves 4
*Preparation time: 5 minutes*
*Cooking time: 10 minutes*
*395 calories per serving*
*Freezing not recommended*

If you love garlic and spicy food then this is your fast-food pasta heaven!

*350 g (12 oz) spaghetti*
*4 garlic cloves, chopped*
*2 tablespoons olive oil*
*2 red chillis, de-seeded and chopped finely or 1 teaspoon dried chilli flakes*
*juice and zest of 1 lemon*
*1 pack of fresh parsley, chopped*
*salt and freshly ground black pepper*

1 Cook the pasta in plenty of salted, boiling water. Drain.

2 Meanwhile heat a large frying-pan or wok and fry the garlic in the olive oil until golden. Add the chillis or chilli flakes and remove the pan from the heat.

3 When the pasta is ready, toss it in the hot oil. Add the lemon juice, zest, chopped parsley, and some seasoning.

## PASTA PUTTANESCA

### POINTS
per serving: 6½          per recipe: 25½

Serves 4
*Preparation time: 5 minutes*
*Cooking time: 10 minutes*
*425 calories per serving*
*Freezing not recommended*

This can be quickly made using store-cupboard ingredients.

*350 g (12 oz) pasta*
*low-fat cooking spray*
*2 garlic cloves, crushed or chopped finely*
*1 fresh chilli, de-seeded and chopped finely, or ½ teaspoon dried chilli flakes*
*55 g (2 oz) canned anchovies, drained and washed*
*175 g (6 oz) pitted black olives, chopped roughly*
*2 tablespoons currants or raisins*
*2 tablespoons tomato purée*
*1 tablespoon capers, rinsed and drained*
*1 teaspoon sugar*
*1 pack of fresh basil, chopped*
*salt and freshly ground black pepper*

1 Cook the pasta in plenty of boiling, salted water. Drain.

2 Spray a large frying-pan with the cooking spray and put it on a medium heat. Fry the garlic until just going golden. Add all the ingredients except for the pasta and basil. Cook for 2 minutes.

3 Toss with the pasta and fresh basil.

**Creamy Smoked Mackerel Pasta: simplicity itself to make.**

## CREAMY SMOKED MACKEREL PASTA

### POINTS
per serving: 8½          per recipe: 35

Serves 4
*Preparation time: 5 minutes*
*Cooking time: 10 minutes*
*530 calories per serving*
*Freezing not recommended*

*240 g (8½ oz) pasta*
*325 g (11½ oz) smoked mackerel, flaked*
*4 tablespoons half-fat crème fraîche*
*1 pack of fresh parsley, chopped*
*salt and freshly ground black pepper*

1 Cook the pasta in plenty of boiling, salted water. Drain.

2 Toss the pasta with the other ingredients and serve.

Pasta
Puttanesca: a
spicy, robust
sauce from the
back streets of
Naples.

**Italian Sardine Pasta: a quick, piquant and healthy pasta recipe.**

## WATERCRESS AND BLUE CHEESE PASTA

**POINTS**

per serving: 6          per recipe: 25

 Serves 4

*Preparation time: 5 minutes*
*Cooking time: 10 minutes*
*415 calories per serving*
*Freezing not recommended*

This recipe uses a little strong flavoured Danish Blue cheese, so you get all the flavour with less of the Points.

*350 g (12 oz) pasta*
*50 g (1¾ oz) Danish Blue cheese*
*100 g (3½ oz) low-fat soft cheese*
*4 tablespoons skimmed milk*
*175 g (6 oz) watercress, chopped roughly*
*salt and freshly ground black pepper*

1 Cook the pasta in plenty of boiling, salted water. Drain.
2 Meanwhile put the cheeses and milk in a large pan and heat, gently stirring, until they are smoothly combined and melted.
3 Toss the pasta with the sauce and watercress and season.

## ITALIAN SARDINE PASTA

**POINTS**

per serving: 5½          per recipe: 23

Serves 4

*Preparation time: 5 minutes*
*Cooking time: 10 minutes*
*440 calories per serving*
*Freezing not recommended*

*350 g (12 oz) pasta*
*2 x 120 g cans sardines in brine*
*250 g (9 oz) cherry tomatoes, halved*
*juice and zest of 1 lemon*
*1 red chilli, de-seeded and chopped finely*
*1 pack of fresh basil, chopped*
*salt and freshly ground black pepper*

1 Cook the pasta in plenty of boiling, salted water. Drain.
2 Meanwhile heat a large pan and add the sardines, tomatoes, lemon juice and zest, chilli and seasoning. Heat through gently for 4 minutes and then toss with the cooked pasta and fresh basil.

## COTTAGE CHEESE AND TOMATO PASTA

**POINTS**

per serving: 6          per recipe: 24

 Serves 4

*Preparation time: 5 minutes*
*Cooking time: 10 minutes*
*415 calories per serving*
*Freezing not recommended*

A lovely low-fat but creamy sauce with fresh flavours.

*350 g (12 oz) pasta*
*300 g (10½ oz) plain cottage cheese*
*4 ripe tomatoes, skinned, de-seeded and chopped*
*4 sun-dried tomatoes, chopped finely*
*½ teaspoon ground nutmeg*
*1 pack of fresh basil or parsley, chopped*
*salt and freshly ground black pepper*

1 Cook the pasta in plenty of salted, boiling water. Drain.
2 Gently heat the cottage cheese in a saucepan and stir in the fresh and sun-dried tomatoes. Add the nutmeg and some seasoning.
3 Toss the pasta with the sauce and sprinkle with fresh basil or parsley.

## SPINACH AND GARLIC PASTA

### POINTS

per serving: 6        per recipe: 25

 *Serves 4*

*Preparation time: 5 minutes*

*Cooking time: 10 minutes*

*450 calories per serving*

*Freezing not recommended*

This recipe is outrageously easy and yet satisfying and healthy.

---

*350 g (12 oz) pasta*

*500 g (1 lb 2 oz) spinach, fresh or frozen and defrosted*

*2 tablespoons pine kernels (optional)*

*100 g (10½ oz) Roulé Light with garlic and parsley*

*salt and freshly ground black pepper*

1  Cook the pasta in plenty of boiling, salted water. Drain.

2  Remove any thick stems from fresh spinach and chop. If using frozen spinach, chop it.

3  Toast the pine kernels under the grill.

4  Add the spinach and cheese to the hot pasta and toss. Season and sprinkle with pine kernels.

---

## CRISPY TURKEY RASHER PASTA

### POINTS

per serving: 5        per recipe: 20½

*Serves 4*

*Preparation time: 10 minutes*

*Cooking time: 10 minutes*

*390 calories per serving*

*Freezing not recommended*

---

*350 g (12 oz) pasta*

*150 g (5½ oz) turkey rashers*

*salt and freshly ground black pepper*

---

FOR THE SALSA

*2 green chillis, de-seeded and chopped finely*

*1 green pepper, de-seeded and chopped finely*

*1 onion, chopped finely*

*125 g can chopped tomatoes*

*2 teaspoons sugar*

*1 tablespoon white wine vinegar*

1  Cook the pasta in plenty of boiling, salted water. Drain.

2  Meanwhile grill the turkey rashers until crispy – 1 minute on each side – then slice into bite-sized pieces.

3  In a bowl mix together all the salsa ingredients with some seasoning. Toss with the cooked pasta and the turkey rashers. Check the seasoning and serve.

**Crispy Turkey Rasher Pasta:** lean and crispy turkey rashers are tossed with a hot Texan salsa and pasta for a tasty, fast supper.

Spicy Prawn Noodles: a little taste of the Orient.

## TASTY NOODLES AND VEGETABLES

**POINTS**

per serving: 3          per recipe: 13

 Serves 4

*Preparation time: 10 minutes*
*Cooking time: 10 minutes*
*300 calories per serving*
*Freezing not recommended*

A light, fragrant meal that can be on the table in minutes.

*250 g (9 oz) noodles*
*low-fat cooking spray*
*2 garlic cloves, sliced finely*
*2.5 cm (1-inch) piece root ginger, peeled and diced finely*
*1 head broccoli, cut into florets*
*2 red peppers, de-seeded and cut into bite-sized pieces*
*100 g (3½ oz) baby corn, cut into bite-sized pieces*
*2 tablespoons plum sauce*
*150 ml (¼ pint) vegetable stock*
*1 pack of fresh coriander or parsley, chopped*

1  Cook the noodles as directed on the packet. Drain.

2  Spray a large frying-pan or wok with the cooking spray and put it on a high heat. Stir-fry the garlic and ginger for 2 minutes, then add the vegetables and stir-fry for another 4 minutes or until they have started to brown at the edges. Add the plum sauce and stock and bring to the boil.

3  Stir in the noodles and fresh coriander or parsley and serve.

## SPICY PRAWN NOODLES

**POINTS**

per serving: 4½          per recipe: 19

Serves 4

*Preparation time: 10 minutes*
*Cooking time: 10 minutes*
*365 calories per serving*
*Freezing not recommended*

*250 g (9 oz) noodles*
*low-fat cooking spray*
*2.5 cm (1-inch) piece fresh ginger, peeled and cut into matchsticks*
*2 garlic cloves, sliced finely*
*400 g (14 oz) cooked, peeled prawns, fresh or frozen*
*1 red chilli, de-seeded and chopped finely*
*450 g (1 lb) baby spinach or bok choy, chopped roughly*
*1 tablespoon soy sauce*
*juice of 1 lemon*

1  Cook the noodles in plenty of salted, boiling water. Drain.

2  Spray a large frying-pan or wok with the cooking spray and put on a medium heat. Stir-fry the ginger and garlic for 2 minutes. Add the prawns, chilli, spinach or bok choy, soy sauce and lemon juice and stir-fry another 4 minutes.

3  Toss with the cooked noodles and serve.